THE
SHIFT

Cover design by: Todd Petelle
Cover photo by: Andrew van Tilborgh

ISBN: 978-1-969062-06-3   1 2 3 4 5 6 7 8 9 10

Printed in the United States of America

STUDY GUIDE

THE
SHIFT

JOHNNY H. MOORE

AVAIL

CONTENTS

FOREWORD BY DR. BENNY TATE

THE
SHIFT

CREATING AN ENVIRONMENT
FOR TRANSFORMATION

JOHNNY H. MOORE

INTRODUCTION

He wants His church to be "an
exceedingly great army."

REFLECT AND TAKE ACTION:

As you read Introduction in *The SHIFT*, reflect on, and respond to the text by answering the following questions.

Where do you see God already at work transforming lives within your church community? What signs of renewal or growth give you hope?

_____

_____

_____

_____

_____

_____

_____

_____

How can small acts—like offering a meal, a listening ear, or a seat at the table—become catalysts for genuine spiritual transformation?

_____

_____

_____

_____

_____

_____

_____

_____

> *"Then He said to me, 'Prophesy to the breath, prophesy, son of man, and say to the breath, "Thus says the Lord GOD, 'Come from the four winds, O breath, and breathe on these slain, that they come to life.'"' So I prophesied as He commanded me, and the breath came into them, and they came to life and stood on their feet, an exceedingly great army."*
>
> **—Ezekiel 37:9-10**

Consider the scripture above and answer the following questions:

What part of your life or ministry feels like "dry bones" right now—lifeless, scattered, or hopeless—and what would it look like for God to breathe new life into that place?

_____

_____

_____

_____

_____

Ezekiel was commanded to prophesy to the breath—to speak life into what was dead. Where is God asking you to boldly speak life, hope, or truth into your church's culture, even if it feels uncomfortable or resisted?

_____

_____

_____

_____

_____

What small "little changes" might God be prompting in your church that could lead to something much greater?

_____

_____

_____

_____

_____

_____

_____

_____

_____

_____

What "graves" of complacency, fear, or comfort might need to be opened in your church for transformation to take root?

_____

_____

_____

_____

_____

_____

_____

_____

_____

_____

Many churches today are plateaued or declining. In what ways could a renewed commitment to Spirit-led transformation—not just better programs or friendlier spaces—help your church move forward again?

_____

_____

_____

_____

_____

_____

_____

_____

_____

_____

What do you hope to gain from this study guide, and what
changes do you long to see in your church as a result?

_____

_____

_____

_____

_____

_____

_____

_____

_____

_____

THE DREAM

A God-ordained SHIFT doesn't happen by accident; it's intentional.

REFLECT AND TAKE ACTION:

As you read Chapter 1: "The Dream" in *The SHIFT*, reflect on, and respond to the text by answering the following questions.

Before engaging with this book, how would you have defined or described what real transformation looks like in a church or in your own life?

_____

_____

_____

_____

_____

_____

_____

God's word in the dream was simple: "All you need is a shift." What shift in perspective, structure, or priorities is your church resisting that could unlock a harvest?

_____

_____

_____

_____

_____

_____

_____

> *"Truly, truly, I say to you, unless a grain of wheat falls into the earth and dies, it remains alone; but if it dies, it bears much fruit. He who loves his life loses it, and he who hates his life in this world will keep it to life eternal. If anyone serves Me, he must follow Me; and where I am, there My servant will be also; if anyone serves Me, the Father will honor him.".*
>
> **—John 12:24-26**

Consider the scripture above and answer the following questions:

What "grain of wheat" in your life or leadership is God asking you to let die so that greater fruit can grow?

_____

_____

_____

_____

_____

_____

_____

In what ways has clinging to comfort, recognition, or control kept you from following Jesus into new levels of fruitfulness?

_____

_____

_____

_____

_____

_____

_____

How does your church's culture of service—or lack of it—reveal whether it is following Christ?

_____

_____

_____

_____

_____

_____

How have you handled seasons where God seemed slow to move, and what did those seasons reveal about your faith?

_____

_____

_____

_____

_____

_____

When was the last time your church embraced a God-given SHIFT instead of clinging to the patterns of the past? What was the outcome?

_____

_____

_____

_____

_____

_____

The chapter describes SHIFT as something intentional, not accidental. How are you preparing your church to be ready when God moves quickly?

_____

_____

_____

_____

_____

_____

In what ways might your church appear active and full on the surface but be missing the deeper movement of God's Spirit? How does this image challenge the way you think about spiritual renewal?

_____

_____

_____

_____

_____

_____

_____

Where might your church's rhythms, priorities, or systems reveal that your church is turned inward instead of outward?

_____

_____

_____

_____

_____

_____

If a divine SHIFT occurred in your church tomorrow, what would be the first visible change in the way you serve, welcome, and love people in your community?

_____

_____

_____

_____

_____

_____

S: SPIRITUAL LIFE

Spiritual disciples produce spiritual people who use spiritual gifts to do spiritual things.

REFLECT AND TAKE ACTION:

As you read Chapter 2: "S: Spiritual Life" in *The SHIFT*, reflect on, and respond to the text by answering the following questions.

The chapter reminds us that "everything starts with God." Where in your ministry have you mistakenly started with strategy, programs, or human effort instead of beginning with Him?

_____

_____

_____

_____

_____

_____

_____

How could your church better equip people to connect with God daily—and how would that change the spiritual climate of your congregation?

_____

_____

_____

_____

_____

_____

_____

_____

> "But the fruit of the Spirit is love, joy, peace, patience, kindness, goodness, faithfulness, gentleness, self-control; against such things there is no law. Now those who belong to Christ Jesus have crucified the flesh with its passions and desires. If we live by the Spirit, let us also walk by the Spirit."
>
> **—Galatians 5:22-25**

Consider the scripture above and answer the following questions:

Which fruit of the Spirit is most evident in your life and church right now, and which fruit is most lacking?

_____

_____

_____

_____

_____

_____

Walking by the Spirit is more than private devotion—it shapes our relationships. How healthy are the relationships within your church, and what do they reveal about the level of spiritual transformation taking place in your community?

_____

_____

_____

_____

_____

_____

If your church doubled its commitment to prayer this year, what practical difference would that make in your church's spiritual vitality, unity, and capacity to see genuine transformation—both inside and beyond its walls?

_____

_____

_____

_____

_____

_____

How does the way your church approaches worship communicate its priorities to guests and newcomers?

_____

_____

_____

_____

_____

_____

Who are you accountable to for your own growth, and how are you holding others accountable in love?

_____

_____

_____

_____

_____

_____

_____

_____

Spiritual maturity is measured by transformation, not attendance. Where do you see spiritual immaturity stunting the growth of your congregation, and how might you address it?

_____

_____

_____

_____

_____

_____

_____

_____

_____

Every believer has been given at least one spiritual gift. How well does your church help people discover and deploy their gifts—and what changes could release more people into ministry?

_____

_____

_____

_____

_____

_____

_____

_____

What challenged you most about this chapter, and why? What did you learn, and how do you plan to apply it to your life and church?

_____

_____

_____

_____

_____

_____

_____

_____

H: HOSPITALITY

The reality is, if you will be a blessing, God will see to it that you always receive one.

REFLECT AND TAKE ACTION:

As you read Chapter 3: "H: Hospitality" in *The SHIFT*, reflect on, and respond to the text by answering the following questions.

Where is your church lagging behind in hospitality, and how might that reveal misplaced priorities?

_____

_____

_____

_____

_____

_____

_____

_____

What would it take for your church to become the kind of place people never want to leave?

_____

_____

_____

_____

_____

_____

_____

_____

> *"Be devoted to one another in brotherly love; give preference*
> *to one another in honor; not lagging behind in diligence,*
> *fervent in spirit, serving the Lord; rejoicing in hope,*
> *persevering in tribulation, devoted to prayer, contributing*
> *to the needs of the saints, practicing hospitality."*
>
> **—Romans 12:10-13**

Consider the scripture above and answer the following questions:

How would you describe your church's level of devotion to one another—and how does that devotion (or lack of it) show up in the way you treat guests?

_____

_____

_____

_____

_____

_____

In what ways have you reduced hospitality at your church to a "friendly smile" or greeting? What would it look like for it to become an act of worship, service, and perseverance?

_____

_____

_____

_____

_____

_____

Most churches claim to be "the friendliest church in town," but guests often experience the opposite. How can you gather honest feedback from outsiders about how welcoming your church really is?

_____

_____

_____

_____

_____

One danger the author highlights is being "ingrown." In what ways has your church become more focused on itself than on welcoming those you don't know?

_____

_____

_____

_____

_____

Share a time when you (or someone you know) felt invisible in church. What lessons can your church learn from that?

_____

_____

_____

_____

_____

_____

_____

Where has your church slipped into a "job mentality," and how is that killing the spirit of hospitality?

_____

_____

_____

_____

_____

_____

_____

Every Sunday should be treated like Easter Sunday in terms of preparation and welcome. How would that kind of mindset transform your church's hospitality?

_____

_____

_____

_____

_____

_____

_____

Systems and training are highlighted as keys to sustaining hospitality. What systems does your church currently lack, and how could better preparation prevent guests from slipping through the cracks?

_____

_____

_____

_____

_____

_____

_____

"The only thing you can take with you to heaven is people." How does that truth challenge the way your church invests its time, resources, and attention on Sundays?

_____

_____

_____

_____

_____

_____

_____

I: INTERDEPENDENCE

When one person accepts Jesus into their life on Sunday morning, everybody on the team gets credit for it.

REFLECT AND TAKE ACTION:

As you read Chapter 4: "I: Interdependence" in *The SHIFT*, reflect on, and respond to the text by answering the following questions.

In what ways are you still tempted to operate with a "lone ranger" mindset, and what impact does that have on your church?

_____

_____

_____

_____

_____

_____

_____

_____

Interdependence begins with seeing everybody as important. Who in your church have you overlooked, dismissed, or undervalued, and how can you begin honoring their place in the body?

_____

_____

_____

_____

_____

_____

_____

_____

> *"So that there may be no division in the body, but that the members may have the same care for one another. And if one member suffers, all the members suffer with it; if one member is honored, all the members rejoice with it."*
>
> **—1 Corinthians 12:25-26**

Consider the scripture above and answer the following questions:

How well does your church embody this picture of shared suffering and shared rejoicing? Provide examples.

_____

_____

_____

_____

_____

_____

Where do you see divisions or disconnects in your church body, and how might an overreliance on independence—rather than interdependence—be causing them?

_____

_____

_____

_____

_____

_____

Serving in the wrong area often leads people to quit. How could your church do a better job of helping people discover their gifts and find their right place of ministry?

_____

_____

_____

_____

_____

_____

Interdependence means rallying around a common mission. What is your church's mission, and how clearly do people in your congregation know and own it?

_____

_____

_____

_____

_____

_____

How might your church's culture change if every member treated the mission as their personal responsibility? How could you achieve this in your church?

_____

_____

_____

_____

_____

_____

_____

_____

One danger is pastors micromanaging instead of equipping. How do leadership styles in your church encourage—or discourage—interdependence?

_____

_____

_____

_____

_____

_____

_____

_____

How could your church do a better job of celebrating unseen teams (nursery, parking, cleaning, tech, follow-up, etc.)?

_____

_____

_____

_____

_____

_____

_____

_____

_____

How does your church care for its volunteers spiritually, and what steps are needed to strengthen discipleship for those who serve?

_____

_____

_____

_____

_____

_____

_____

_____

_____

F: FOCUS OUT

If we are going to focus out, we must open the eyes of our hearts to see a hurting world.

REFLECT AND TAKE ACTION:

As you read Chapter 5: "F: Focus Out" in *The SHIFT*, reflect on, and respond to the text by answering the following questions.

Churches can obsess over numbers inside the building while ignoring the greater number of lost people outside. Where has your church fallen into that trap?

_____

_____

_____

_____

_____

_____

_____

In what ways is your church intentionally going where people are, rather than waiting for them to come to you?

_____

_____

_____

_____

_____

_____

_____

> *"Do you not say, 'There are yet four months, and then comes the harvest'? Behold, I say to you, lift up your eyes and look on the fields, that they are white for harvest."*
>
> **—John 4:35**

Consider the scripture above and answer the following questions:

What excuses have you or your church made for waiting instead of acting, and how do they compare with Jesus's words in this passage?

_____

_____

_____

_____

_____

_____

_____

Where do you sense God calling your church to "lift up its eyes" and see people who have been overlooked or ignored?

_____

_____

_____

_____

_____

_____

_____

What needs to change in your perspective, comfort, or schedule for you to truly see the hurting people around you?

_____

_____

_____

_____

_____

_____

What overlooked spaces or resources could your church begin using to connect with your community?

_____

_____

_____

_____

_____

_____

Who in your life might be struggling more deeply today because the church delayed reaching out?

_____

_____

_____

_____

_____

_____

_____

What assumptions about your own community might be limiting your vision of what God can do?

_____

_____

_____

_____

_____

_____

_____

What is one concrete step you can take this week (e.g., inviting, engaging, and serving) to practice focusing out in your church?

_____

_____

_____

_____

_____

_____

_____

_____

_____

The chapter closes by warning against gaining the world but losing your local harvest. How does that truth challenge your church's current priorities and practices?

_____

_____

_____

_____

_____

_____

_____

_____

T: TRANSFORMATION

If the church will love and welcome those nobody wants, God will transform them into people others would die to have.

REFLECT AND TAKE ACTION:

As you read Chapter 6: "T: Transformation" in *The SHIFT*, reflect on, and respond to the text by answering the following questions.

The chapter compares transformation to metamorphosis—the caterpillar becoming a butterfly. Where in your life or church do you see God calling for that kind of radical change?

_____

_____

_____

_____

_____

_____

_____

_____

Where do you see "dry bones" in your church that need God's Spirit to breathe new life?

_____

_____

_____

_____

_____

_____

_____

_____

"And do not be conformed to this world, but be transformed by the renewing of your mind, so that you may prove what the will of God is, that which is good and acceptable and perfect."

—Romans 12:2

Consider the scripture above and answer the following questions:

What areas of your thinking most need renewal so that your life and ministry reflect God's will rather than the world's patterns?

_____

_____

_____

_____

_____

_____

_____

_____

How might hospitality serve as a visible expression of a renewed mind and transformed heart within your congregation?

_____

_____

_____

_____

_____

_____

_____

_____

In what ways do you, like Nicodemus, try to explain spiritual transformation with human reasoning instead of faith?

_____

_____

_____

_____

_____

_____

One sign of transformation is living from the inside out. How would your church look different if it truly drew its identity from God's mission instead of tradition, programs, or numbers?

_____

_____

_____

_____

_____

_____

Another sign is loving from the outside in. How is your church currently expressing love to outsiders, and how could you better welcome those "nobody else wants"?

_____

_____

_____

_____

_____

_____

Transformation is evident when a church labors together instead of spotlighting individuals. Where has competition or credit-seeking hindered ministry in your church?

_____

_____

_____

_____

_____

_____

Think of a recent hardship in your church: did it cause division and fear, or did it deepen dependence on God and unity among His people?

_____

_____

_____

_____

_____

_____

_____

How might recent difficulties in your church actually be preparing you to practice deeper, more Christlike hospitality toward guests, neighbors, or even those who have hurt you?

_____

_____

_____

_____

_____

_____

How is your church preparing to disciple and mobilize those who first experience hospitality at the door, the table, or an event, so that they are welcomed in and then sent back out as witnesses?

_____

_____

_____

_____

_____

_____

CHAPTER 7

CREATING A SHIFT

*It is the pastor's responsibility
to lead the church into a place
where a SHIFT can happen.*

REFLECT AND TAKE ACTION:

As you read Chapter 7: "Creating a SHIFT" in *The SHIFT*, reflect on, and respond to the text by answering the following questions.

A SHIFT doesn't happen overnight but requires intentional preparation. Where has your church been guilty of expecting quick fixes instead of cultivating long-term change?

_____

_____

_____

_____

_____

_____

_____

How might your preaching—or the preaching you hear—need to shift to prepare people for transformation?

_____

_____

_____

_____

_____

_____

_____

> *"From whom the whole body, being fitted and held together by what every joint supplies, according to the proper working of each individual part, causes the growth of the body for the building up of itself in love."*
>
> **—Ephesians 4:16**

Consider the scripture above and answer the following questions:

How does true transformation within the church depend on every member supplying spiritual strength, unity, and purpose to the whole?

_____

_____

_____

_____

_____

_____

What would it look like for your church to grow not just in size, but in love, as Ephesians 4:16 describes?

_____

_____

_____

_____

_____

_____

_____

Many churches aren't ready to focus out because they aren't first grounded in spiritual life, hospitality, or interdependence. Which of these areas is weakest in your church, and how is it holding back growth?

_____

_____

_____

_____

_____

_____

Where has your church assumed people "just know" how to be welcoming, and what could intentional training change?

_____

_____

_____

_____

_____

_____

How could better systems of interdependence and clear training create healthier, longer-lasting service in your church?

_____

_____

_____

_____

_____

_____

Where in your church is the "weakest link" right now, and what specific investment could strengthen it?

_____

_____

_____

_____

_____

_____

How could your church culture shift from doing occasional outreach to living evangelistically every day?

_____

_____

_____

_____

_____

_____

Think of a current challenge in your church; how would viewing it as part of the SHIFT alter your response?

_____

_____

_____

_____

_____

If someone walked into your church today, what evidence would they see that a SHIFT is truly taking place?

_____

_____

_____

_____

_____

Now that you've completed the book and study guide, how has your understanding of transformation—what it looks like, how it begins, and how it spreads—changed? What steps will you take to put this transformation into practice in your church?

_____

_____

_____

_____

_____

www.ingramcontent.com/pod-product-compliance
Lightning Source LLC
Chambersburg PA
CBHW070050100426
42734CB00040B/2975